With Extreme Prejudice

Lest We Forget

Emmett Wheatfall

Kasie,

Imagine with me!

11/21/23

EW

Fernwood
PRESS

With Extreme Prejudice
Lest We Forget

©2022 by Emmett Wheatfall

Fernwood Press
Newberg, Oregon
https://www.fernwoodpress.com

Printed in the United States of America

Cover and page design: Mareesa Fawver Moss

Cover image provided by the Public Health Image Library
from the Centers for Disease Control and Prevention

ISBN 978-1-59498-088-6

for Paul and Sherry Fishman

Table of Contents

We know that the letters of the alphabet are neutral and meaningless until they are combined to make a word which itself has no significance until it is inserted into a sentence and interpreted by those who speak it.

Isabel Wilkerson,
author of *Caste: The Origins of Our Discontents*

Author's Note

With Extreme Prejudice is a euphemism for the execution of a person, particularly an assassination. Without question, COVID-19 ends and injures human lives. It is merciless in carrying out its purpose. Humanity must never forget COVID-19 prosecutes *With Extreme Prejudice.*

Foreword

The truth is I have admired Emmett Wheatfall from the first moment I met him a decade ago. This poet—now three-score-plus-five years wise—lights up a room with his smile, his voice, his open heart, and his expansive mind. This is a poet whose generosity is boundless, whose humility is inspiring, and whose poetry is passionate and accessible. As a poet, Wheatfall does not shy away from the in-your-face-truths audiences near and far need to hear.

With Extreme Prejudice: Lest We Forget is his latest foray into observational truth-telling. This collection bears witness to the early arrival and historicity of the COVID-19 pandemic, which Wheatfall elegantly describes as *The greatest hitchhiker on earth … / making its rounds* ("Every Nation Under The Sun").

In poem after poem, he explores both the ongoing fear of a disease that has taken at least a million lives as well as the hope for that brighter future we all yearn for. The poem, "For All We Lose," sets up this interplay:

> For all we lose,
> never to come again,
> the lighthouse remains,
> the channels flow,
> and humanity
> will go on.

Aware of his own mortality, Wheatfall is not afraid to show his own vulnerability. In "For The Most Part," he lays himself bare:

> For the record, I am a black male
> whose legs continue to grow weak,
> whose knees incessantly throb and ache
> despite Copper Fit compression sleeves.
> Under a thick heating blanket, my toes curl.
> For the most part, I have resigned myself
> to the idea I have not played enough golf.
> On occasion, a shot of bourbon rocks my senses,
> infrequent sex stiffens my joints,
> an 81 mg aspirin tablet—a daily necessity.

And, in typical Wheatfall fashion, the poem lands on an upbeat note: *For the most part, in the sweet by-and-by / I hope to live forever.*

The poet is not only physically vulnerable but also admits to emotional vulnerability. In "World War C," he says, *I am scared, man—oh, how I am scared.* In "Beyond the Shadows," he writes, *We know despair, / and despair knows us.* And, in "Freddy's Stimulus Check,"

> In these the days of COVID-19—
>   the Smiths cannot pay their rent;
> a lawn service mows my lawn.
>   Freddy has not received his stimulus check;
> I periodically reallocate my investments.
>   A homeless family has not eaten;
> Karen and I eat three meals a day. . . .
>   All over the world, people are dying;
> I am alive here in Portland, Oregon.
>   I feel guilty.

How authentic: this fear, despair, and guilt of a poet who was not afraid to share his feelings from the beginning of the pandemic and would attest to them now.

Throughout this collection, Wheatfall surprises us with allusions to Ernest Hemingway, Winston Churchill, Patrick Henry, Leonard Cohen, and Charles Bukowski. He also delights us with unexpected images that emerge from his plain-spoken poems. For example, in "The Man on Earth's Moon," he writes:

> Wait for it.
> Watch for it. Stars will shine again.
> And the man on earth's moon?
> He will look back and smile.

In "This Summer Day,"

> The cowgirl
> wearing cowgirl boots
> is hot-hot on the heels
> of so much fun.

And in "Somewhere Now,"

> a child licks ice cream
> for the first time.

The bottom line of *With Extreme Prejudice: Lest We Forget* is that COVID-19 is no match for hope: three years ago or now. *Eventually, the vagabond will die*, Wheatfall proclaims in "Sing Like Italy." Then,

> seniors will rejoice in mercy that is grace,
> some will visit the gravesite of the less fortunate,
> Sally will again hang washcloths on clotheslines,
> Sam will return to his rickety rocking chair,
> sisters will sob in their mother's arms,
> sons will hug their father.

Wheatfall's poetic honesty reminds me of Galway Kinnell who said, "To me, poetry is somebody standing up ... and saying, with as little concealment as possible, what it is for him or her to be on earth at this moment."

With Extreme Prejudice: Lest We Forget suggests we look back in time—*with as little concealment as possible*—at the poet's observation of the early years of living with COVID-19. He stands up and offers us hard and hopeful truths: the hallmark not of one single poem in this collection but the entire body of Wheatfall's inspiring and captivating work.

Carolyn Martin, Ph.D.
Poetry Editor, *Kosmos Quarterly:*
journal for global transformation

Before the End of Day

Before the end of day comes,
advancing the question, *Where have all the day-birds gone?*
Moreover, where have all the victims of COVID-19 gone?

More and more day-birds flee to somewhere.
More and more victims of COVID-19 descend somewhere,
somewhere beyond end of day.

I wonder if someday I will make my way somewhere—
somewhere beyond the end of day. More and more,
I am sure I will go and never return.

If anyone returns before I go, please let me know—
before end of day?

Beyond the Shadows

Under an avalanche of despair
family members find themselves.

Who is willing to care
other than we, the nation's
healthcare workers?

We know despair,
and despair knows us.

We tell ourselves
we need to stay vigilant,
to cast off our collective fear.

We are not donuts
dipped in hot coffee
offering no complaint.
We are not Pinocchios
with wooden noses
hyper-extended as if lying.

What is to be said of this
frequent visitor named despair
who shows up unannounced?

Despair should knock upon arrival,
reveal itself in the dimly lit foreground,
way beyond the shadows
of moonlit nights.

Light a candle in our honor!
Shake a big stick at COVID-19!

A rooster need not crow like a
circus barker to get our attention.

No choir nor ensemble member
is needed to slap a tambourine to
restore the earthiness of our joy.

Where is your hope, my friends?
Where is our redemption
in this, the era of COVID-19?

Britton Minor

I wish just the two of us could sit
on the edge of the earth—
our legs and feet dangling freely,
the sun setting on the distant horizon
as that mesmerizing version
of Leonard Cohen's *Hallelujah*
plays in the background—while we pray
for peace on earth and goodwill
to all humanity. I dream of this.
Your friend,
Emmett

Charles Bukowski Might Say

Who would write a poem right now
while sheltering in place?
"Every *goddamn* poet I know"—
something poet Charles Bukowski might say,
and he's been long since dead now.
Damn it! I'm writing one right now.
Gee, COVID-19!

COVID-19

You scourge:
obscure,
unspoken,
like silent words.
My lungs collapse
like trees felled
by men. Imagine a
piece of petrified bone
taken from an
ancient sarcophagus.
What must you be
to that end, then?
Obscure?

Dying in the Shadow of Pandemic

Dying in the shadow of pandemic and the plight of coronavirus is
like missing cartilage in the human knee. Humanity aches for mobility.
We are bowed right now; we are reeds bending in the wind.
Who thought we could be humbled, brought to our collective knees,
sustained only by the possibilities of modern medicine and the self-
sacrifice of professional healers? Some look to the cross, others to
thought and prayer, many to the probability of chance. Humanity
should lower her nose a little, expel the breath in her bosom inflating
her sense of pride, recognize how there are things in this world that
take the shine off her crown. Later than sooner, humanity will rise
to stand again, lest she forget earthly humility and seize the day.

Every Nation Under the Sun

      One person transmitted the virus
to someone else. That person who transmitted the virus
and that someone else
      began infecting others.
                       As a result,
others in cities, towns, villages,
and hamlets contracted the coronavirus.
      Quickly, the entire state became unwitting
recipients.
      Now, every nation under the sun
has asymptomatic carriers of the virus.
The greatest hitchhiker on earth
is making its rounds.

For All We Lose

COVID-19

For all we lose,
never to come again,
the lighthouse remains,
the channels flow,
and humanity
will go on.

For the Most Part

For the most part, I am still here.
Threescore plus five years have passed,
meaning: I am 65 years old.

For the record, I am a black male
whose legs continue to grow weak,
whose knees incessantly throb and ache
despite Copper Fit compression sleeves.
Under a thick heating blanket, my toes curl.
For the most part, I have resigned myself
to the idea I have not played enough golf.
On occasion, a shot of bourbon rocks my senses,
infrequent sex stiffens my joints,
an 81 mg aspirin tablet—a daily necessity.

My black hair follicles are silver-gray now;
the vision I once had—subsiding.
My memory is the epitome of lost megabytes.
At least this big penis of mine retains its rigidity.

Another year will come,
meaning: I will be 65 years old.
I am fearful of COVID-19.
For the most part, in the sweet by-and-by,
I hope to live forever.

Freddy's Stimulus Check

In these the days of COVID-19—
      the Smiths cannot pay their rent;
a lawn service mows my lawn.
      Freddy has not received his stimulus check;
I periodically reallocate my investments.
      A homeless family has not eaten;
Karen and I eat three meals a day.
      Saundra is sheltering at home alone;
my family communicates daily.
      An acquaintance is fearful and nervous;
I admonished her to *be safe, smart, and vigilant.*
      A dear friend telephoned me this morning;
I awoke intent on telephoning him.
      People are asking, *Where is God?*
My gospel song continues to get airplay.
      Confidence in elected officials is waning;
humanity needs faith, hope, and love.
      All over the world, people are dying;
I'm alive here in Portland, Oregon.
      I feel guilty.

Go Into the Woods

Should I go into the woods?
I am told there are no people there.
      I come from people who were bold.
I should go into the woods.
It is hard being the last generation,
      this sensitive generation unnerving.
As a man over 60, I am scared.
The trees here remind me of tall men,
      men I looked up to early in life—
all of them befallen by coronavirus.
I am sounding the warning—do not
      go into the woods, you widowers.
Sitting on this stump
reminds me of the men who once
      worked here.

Hemingway Would Have Taken Me Fishing

Is the end of my wit this driveway?
It will be if I don't let go of this steering column.
Is this how an overweight lemon branch feels,
        dangling with tongue-tingling tanginess?
My body leans forward like a tree blown in the wind.
If only I had been Ernest Hemingway's friend.
Hemingway would have taken me fishing—
not giving a damn, we would have drank his best liquor.
That is what I imagine.
For the death of me—climbing steps to my front door,
the Great Wall of China preferable.
It would represent something newly engaged.
If only I had not come of age; wherefore,
        I would lose myself in a Hardy Boys mystery,
even a Nancy Drew or two.
Those days have rolled out to sea,
        driven by the silver moon's dictates.
I would dance a soft-shoe for duct-tape.
Is there anything better to hold together
        the discordant thoughts of an unfurling wit?
Take to viewing this evening's news?
Another report about COVID-19?
Should I?

I Can Only Imagine

A blade of grass lay freshly cut.
Other blades
     will lie down beside me.
Subject to manicure every blade.
This is something incontrovertible.
So, at that appointed day,
     I will lie down next to my father
     and near my mother.
     Might I precede my eldest sister?
Some say I will return again;
wherefore,
     life is a journey back
          to where you started from.
I cannot say for certain what that means.
If I am cut down though,
I do hope I am buried
     deep within the depths of love
          in these the days of COVID-19.

I Will

COVID-19 is saying,

I will take

from you your sunshine as well as your rain,
the freedom that is your liberty, the livelihood that keeps
you and yours living; eventually, the moments you deny others
will belong to someone else, even retail stores, motels, and
hotels, corporate offices, and commercial property;
as well as your homes, cabins, and beach houses, your
children's education at colleges and universities,
your local, regional, and national sporting
events, public and private gatherings, your way of life,
your social networking, your forms of government, your economic
prowess. And when the beer on tap runs dry, you will then
find a vaccine and reminisce about the life you once knew.
Just know the following: a new form of COVID-19
will come, saying,

I will take

I Would Whisper

During COVID-19,
it was a kiss,
more than one to say the least,
gender discrimination
not a factor. Afterward, caressing,
you wanted more
and visited again and again.
The imprint, pressing
of skin, deposits of sheer bliss,
ruby colored blemishes—
I would whisper, *kiss me.*

If I Die Because of COVID-19

I will love the mourning of the evening of my passing.
The sun will not have failed me;
the warmth of noonday will have complimented all the wildflowers.
They will grace the dirt mound that is monument to my having existed
and the grave cradling the darkness that swaddles me.
The memories at sunset make this new world my home
given how all the shadows in my life have faded.

If Only There Were Peace on Earth

A lament derived from the perspective
of "Hark! the Herald Angels Sing."

Hark! is seldom heard.
If only we could hear the angels sing.
Upheaval reigns on earth—
God forbid,
not another newborn king.
—God and COVID-19,
please reconcile.

If Tomorrow Should Be the Day

Autumn—good morning.
Winter, spring, summer, and fall—
all are away on call,
      seeing you here
           arrayed in gorgeous colors.
      I phoned with glee my mother—
she was giddy as can be
seeing yellow, green, and ruby-colored leaves,
fully blossomed neighborhood trees,
      squirrels pesky,
          fowl squawking in trees.
      Autumn's aromatic smell
         while quarantined:
Today is my 87th, mother says.
If today is the day I die
in the beauty of autumn, let me lie
      as if a young child.
      Then she let loose a sigh.
         I knew then
            I needed to leave her right there;
      I waxed stronger with a smile and a prayer,
saying within myself, *I love you, Mom.*
Eventually, I returned to carriage the phone,
then reveled at autumn,
      sheltering at home alone.

If You Were Me

If you were me,
I would love you
like a tree in my forest,
having fallen for me.

I would catch you in my forest.
I would always let you fall ever so softly
upon me in my forest.

In the days of COVID-19,
love would not go quietly into the night.
I would be you—everything
obscured by the love that is me.

If you were me,
I would love you
like a tree in my forest,
having fallen for me.

I would love you
if you were me
and I were you.

No, Not the Beer

a white or colored circle or set of
concentric circles of light seen around
a luminous body, especially around
the sun or moon

    Dictionary.com

Corona? No, not the beer. And not the epigraph above. The virus.
That indomitable coronavirus. It is not a respecter of persons.
Coronavirus holds no regard for ethnicity, gender,
sexual orientation; not sparing the elderly, the poor,
the marginalized, especially children. Coronavirus thumbs its nose
at virologists, epidemiologists, kings, monarchs, tyrants, and dictators;
even the sanctimonious president of the United States. God forbid
Grupo Modelo halts production of Corona beer. I know Corona beer
to be a thirst quencher and certainly not a life taker.
Bottoms up and hearty cheers for Grupo Modelo Corona beer.

Not Another World War

> never give in, never give in,
> never, never, never, never—in nothing,
> great or small, large, or petty—
> never give in except to convictions
> of honor and good sense
>
> —Winston Churchill

If COVID-19 is another World War,
some people will not outlive their bunkers.
In this war, sheltering in place is most notable—
many will endure,
others grumble.
We must never forget
that there is no such thing as collateral damage.
        Therefore,
a casualty of this war your neighbor may become.
Look to the cross.
Look to the Red Cross.
Look to your neighbor across the street.
Look out for your neighbors lining the street.
Go to him.
        Go to her.
                Go to them.

For if there is any humanity in you, help him, her, and them.
Possess god-like regard for the children of this war.
And you, the wise, consider your elders,
and let benevolence validate your empathy.
Be safe.
> Be smart.
>> Be fierce.
>>> Be vigilant and sober.
For here now is the COVID-19
World War.

Pandemic

Nonexistent before emboldened conception,
out of the dank unknown to life you spring.
Unheralded your seminal arrival—except for
that first snatching away of breath
                              that announced your birth.
The yellow sun,
that crescent moon,
twinkling celestial stars
            spoke not a word;
wild winds,
torrential rain,
provincial fires
            remain mute.
Our universe remains
                  strangely silent—
the creator our absentee curator.
Swaddled in the invisible you come,
            COVID-19.
To the expanse you fling yourself,
hitching a ride like a vagabond.
Neither man nor woman are you;
from humanity came not one summons,
not a single writ.
You have seized upon our existence.
The author of unsanctioned liberty
cloaked as the essence of Grim Reaper,
initiating this era of reaping and sowing
like a man going around taking names.
For the field of humanity is fertile;
your virility impregnating.
You will never be our panacea.

Some describe you as epidemic.
There is more to you than epidemic.
Pandemic? Yes! Pandemic!
Whereby you seize upon old oak trees,
old trees touched by disease
that no longer bloom nor bear blossoms,
inconsistent among adolescents,
merciful to the tender shoot.
There are insufficient tests;
in your cunning you test us.
We the People of this world
must place our neighbor before ourselves—
the elderly being our image and destiny—
actualize our desire to survive,
to secure the future for our posterity.
For we will prevail.
We must.

Rarely if Ever

We were hospitalized.
I went home.
You died.

We were hospitalized. Rarely if ever
is a slap to the face anticipated, but its
sting can last beyond 14 days.

That hospital is where I recovered.
However, it is where you died.
Neither of us had time to figure.

You are blessed. The life I am living
will continue, attention to healthy living
a must. You rest in peace and place.

We were hospitalized.
I went home.
You died.

Remember Me

More than less,
I love you.
If not for
the benevolence of a woman,
every dream has its end.
Cheers to the next thousand years.
I know this is sudden,
albeit, given the coronavirus—
if ever I face this again,
I will scent the note,
seal it with a kiss.
It will be yours for a witness
        if ever
you remember me.

Sanctuary

Access to beaches denied,
to the river—a no-go.
Park visits prohibited,
to-go food a no-go.
Athletes cannot play ball,
social media now the show
during COVID-19.
My patio—
      sanctuary!

Sing Like Italy

Spring is coming.
Songbirds will return to trees,
smoke will rise from barbecue pits,
Sunday School will welcome back children,
Saturday markets will bustle with customers,
so will songs about the Savior be sung by church choirs.

Eventually, the vagabond will die—

seniors will rejoice in mercy that is grace,
some will visit the gravesite of the less fortunate,
Sally will again hang washcloths on clotheslines,
Sam will return to his rickety rocking chair,
sisters will sob in their mother's arms,
sons will hug their father.

In the skyline rests our lives.
Until our deliverance comes,
let us gaze unselfishly at essential workers
and sing like Italy.

Social Distancing

A lone dove takes to flight.
The terminology of the day: "Shelter in Place."
A quarrel or two seems insufficient for a gaggle;
social distancing more than a hop, skip, and jump.
During quarantine, I chew Dentyne gum.
I will not succumb from a lack of food or water;
I am overwhelmed by the silence.

Somewhere Now

Before the virus
when death came,
what was known

died.

Somewhere now,
a child licks ice cream
for the first time.

The King Is Dead

Rows and rows of empty seats.
Where have all the theater-goers gone?
The orchestral pit an empty lot;
I'm told Broadway is as silent as death.
Coronavirus, the current off-Broadway play—
I hear the whole world is its stage.
Like Greek tragedies, most everyone dies,
therefore, no thespian is willing to perform.
There are only roles for the dead and dying;
this playwright is no intellectual
and never the ardent fiction writer.
Neither is this visionary a teller of tall tales;
in this drama, no one shouts, "Long live the king!"
After the final curtain call, when houselights dim,
audiences will never forget,

    "The king is dead! The king is dead!"

The Man on Earth's Moon

In satisfying sunlight,
      who can think quarantine?
A call from the wild, enticing.
The wilderness, emancipating.
A cabin in the woods, enchanting.
Any trickling brook
      an entrance into mindfulness.
Meditations by John Brehm
      worthy of anticipation.

Take to sitting on a tree stump.
Sing with the singing Whippoorwills.
Wait for baby squirrels to scurry
      across tree branches. Do marvel
        at the twinkling light
          piercing
              the limbs of tall trees.

      Wait for it.
Watch for it. Stars will shine again.
And the man on earth's moon?
He will look back and smile.

The President Did Not Conscript You

The president did not conscript you,
nor did the U.S. military recruit you.
No terrorist placed a gun to your head and made you;
not a known or unknown militia coerced you—
essential worker,
our nation's citizen soldier,
dedicated warrior:
bold, brave, fierce.
You hold the line.
You stem the tide of tidal wave
in this, the COVID-19 World War.

This is not the fictional Clone War.
This is the *real* Clone War.
Such a stealthy enemy, who multiplies and survives,
who lays low and reaches high,
taking the last of breath away
from the elderly in nursing homes every day.
A lot of healthy men and women
have experienced life's beginning
only to die long before their natural ending,
ravishing communities as if predestined
for doom. Forget not the loss of babies
coming soon.

The Sound of Silence

From within my mouth extends an oak tree.
Fowl from the air have taken to rest upon its branches.
This happens to be nothing unusual—except for
the oak tree extending from within my mouth.
It's as if I have called a meeting of the airy.
Perched, upper levels, are soaring birds who sing soprano.
Mid-level branches sustain petite birds with alto voices.
Perched below are crows who sing tenor and bass.
If not for my mouth, if not for the extending oak tree,
the sound of silence would rule the day. So sing!
Sing!

This Summer Day

This summer day,
this hot-hot summer day,
this dude ranch is buzzing.
This wild sense of freedom rules the day.
In truth,
not long ago—
part of an enduring history
before the coronavirus arrived—
there were things to be rode
where *hold on tight* was necessary.
The cowgirl
wearing cowgirl boots
is hot-hot on the heels
of so much fun.

When a Poet Dies

When a lily fades,
      another will shine.
When a poet dies,
      another will rise.
Life and death
      are in the dying
and the rising.
      If COVID-19 takes me,
other poets will rise.

When It's Over

During COVID-19,
blue jays will still be blue,
the sky above a light blue,
playing somewhere—the blues.
A child will feel blue.
My favorite color is blue.
Blue are oceans beyond shorelines.
Elvis—Blue Suede Shoes.
Best beer ever—Blue Moon.
Everyone will smile again,
Dear Lord—soon.

Will the Blue Jay Change Color?

At the behest of scourge,
fallen to his death
upon a bed of green grass,
his temporal resting place—
will the blue jay change color?
Over time, he will,
as will some human beings
if the bed of grass
where they lay last
is not cordoned off, and a stone
set forth in memoriam,
whereupon inscribed is a
name, date of birth, date
of death—never the reason being
a death from COVID-19.

Winter Is Coming!

Winter is coming! Not the seasonal one.
Flakes unending, snow pending, to no end
apprehending. Buds dying on vines, the weight
of burden unbearable. You be your brother's keeper;
you be your kinsmen's redeemer. Be pandemic
ending. Winter is coming!

With Extreme Prejudice

Bodacious is their bravado.
Antithetical in principle is the converse
strolling in the midst of rally-rousing-ruckus,
armed with assault rifles, arrayed in camouflage,
amid protesters shouting, "Black Lives Matter!"
on the steps leading to the state capitol.

In the gaggle is heard Patrick Henry's,

> *Give me liberty or give me death!*

This is not the American Revolution!
Now is the deadly time of COVID-19.
We who are watching from a distance understand,

> *Give me liberty or give me death!*

Is this not the time when we should wear a mask,
wash our hands, social distance, and love our neighbor?
How might we reconcile liberty considering COVID-19?
Is liberty any freer than the eternal bond of death,
knowing said liberty will have sanctioned said death—

with extreme prejudice?

World War C

How long will you listen to Trump's doom?
He is neither an ancient of old nor a renowned sage.
His pronouncements are blackberries bereft of wine,
      prognostications without merit or earthly foundation.
Of them, how long will you pander to his make-believe?
Who are they that can make sense of these times?
More and more, Trump's visions entrap the gullible;
      chance and probability speak with less certainty.
Many share his panacea for enriched embellishment.
Who among you craves sourdough more than sweetbread?
Give yourself a hardline to science and the experts
      in this, the time of COVID-19.
I am scared, man—oh, how I am scared.

Write a Letter

During COVID-19

Have you thought of this? Write a letter. Use snail mail.
Use the U.S. Postal Service servicing your zip code.

Write the letter using your own hand. If you cannot write,
get a youngster to write it for you. Be patient; teach
that kid how to write cursive.

With your own hand, try a fountain pen. If interested in
trying something new, use a quill tip with black ink.
Dip and write until you master its use.

Do not forget to sign the letter. Do not forget to lightly
spray a sweet perfume on it. Fold it in thirds, place it in a
letter-size envelope, and lick it like you would your lover.

Seal it.

Walk it to your post office box at the end of your driveway,
or place it in the outside mailbox at the Post Office. Better yet,
hand it to your mail carrier, then say,

Thank you!

Wait for a reply like you would the return of a pigeon carrier.
You never know—a reply may come by way of pigeon. Be sure
to say,

Thank you

by leaving some breadcrumbs for that
wonderful commissioned civil servant.

WWJD

What would Jesus do?

What would Jesus do in these days of COVID-19?
Would Jesus show the world how his love could end
the suffering blanketing the earth,
bring about the cleansing of everyone virally infected,
and unmask the false sages doubting the virility of COVID-19?
Might he declare unashamedly empirical truth, resurrect
dead hopes and dreams, notwithstanding the poor
in spirit by virtue of his good deeds?

Would Jesus do that?

Year 2020

In the days before 2020, high hopes were in play.
My personal style mattered. Unforeseen was the arrival
of the facemask. There was a time when a facemask
would be contextualized in some sort of satirical framework.
I do not think I'm alone in this thinking. I had envisioned
a totally different wardrobe.

Is anything more timeless than fashion?
As I write, I wonder if this will be the new normal.
All my choices were predicated on 2020. There is still a tendency
for me to debate that with myself; obviously, it will be done
in private. While almost oblivious to vanity, I say this with an
unfussy modesty: in hindsight, my personal style matters.

Title Index

W

Y

First Line Index